BITING POINT

by Sid Sagar

Biting Point was first performed at the Fruit Market multi-storey car park in Hull on 10 May 2025, before touring to car parks in Grimsby, Pocklington, Selby, Beverley, Redcar and Bridlington.

Cast

John	Marc Graham
Anita	Katie Singh
Voice Actors	Sudha Bhuchar
	Emma Bright
	Jack Chamberlain
	Sophie Clay
	Emilio Encinoso-Gil
	Amelia Grimes
	Elle Ideson
	Tony Jayawardena
	Dan McGarry
	Laura Meredith
	Chris Pearson
	Oliver Strong

Creative and Production Team

Writer	Sid Sagar
Sensitivity Reader	Jay Mitra
Director	Paul Smith
Assistant Director	Grace Waga Glevey
Dramaturg	Matthew May
Designer	Bethany Wells
Sound Designer	Tom Smith
Movement Director	Danielle Clements
Composer	Kobby Taylor
Keys	Vivek Santhosh
Lighting Designer	Caitlin Clarke
Audience Experience Director	Rachael Abbey
Artistic Collaborators	Jay Mitra
	Grace Waga Glevey
Producer	Sarah Penney
Production Manager	Danielle Harris
Company Stage Manager	Shona Wright
Deputy Stage Manager	Olivia Dudley
Technical Stage Manager	Caitlin Clarke
Sound Engineer	Jack Pellatt
BSL Interpreter (Hull)	Dave Wycherley
PR	Mobius

Local Ambassadors Patrick Hollifield
Louise Record
Megan Waite

Biting Point is written by Sid Sagar and produced by Middle Child, funded by Arts Council England, Hull City Council, Garfield Weston Foundation and Sylvia Waddilove, supported by Pocklington Arts Centre, East Riding of Yorkshire Council, Selby Town Hall, Redcar and Cleveland Borough Council, The Culture House Grimsby and Wykeland.

Biting Point was developed through the Without Walls Blueprint R&D with the support of the National Theatre Generate Programme, The Mono Box, Davina Moss, Tessa Walker, Jennifer Davis and Roy Williams.

Middle Child would like to thank the following people for their participation in the R&D process at the National Theatre Studio: Rachael Abbey, Sophie Clay, Marc Graham, Ellie Leaver, Dan McGarry, Laura Meredith, Jay Mitra, Tom Smith, Manjinder Virk and Bethany Wells.

Cover illustration by Lily Blakely and title artwork by Hatch Hull.

Middle Child are a new writing theatre company rooted in Hull.

We bring people together for unforgettable experiences full of big ideas. Every day we work towards a fair and equitable world where anyone's story can be told and heard. We commission the writers of tomorrow to tell untold stories that make sense of the world today.

We set fire to expectations of what a night at the theatre can be. From electrifying gig theatre in Hull nightclubs to drag-inspired cabaret in London and family shows in Salford parks, we deliver unmissable performances in unexpected places.

Our award-winning work is underpinned by our commitment to investing in local people, providing opportunity without having to leave the city. From Fresh Ink: Hull Playwriting Festival to our Theatre Library and renowned workshop programme, we provide accessible routes into the industry.

We always prioritise wellbeing, in the stories we tell, the artists we develop and the people we employ. The social value of increasing access to great art drives everything we do.

Middle Child are a registered charity, an Arts Council England national portfolio organisation and receive significant support from Hull City Council and the Garfield Weston Foundation. We are the resident company of the National Theatre and are generously supported by our Middle Child Mates.

> "[Fresh Ink is] addressing the crisis in new writing and the lack of opportunity for writers. Middle Child is taking action and proving that when there is no opportunity, companies and theatres can make it. If they choose to do so."
>
> Lyn Gardner, *The Stage*

Middle Child

Artistic Director and CEO	Paul Smith
Executive Director	Emily Anderton
Senior Producer	Sarah Penney
Audience Development Manager	Jamie Potter
General and Production Manager	Danielle Harris
Literary Manager	Matthew May
Marketing Assistant	Alice Beaumont

Founding Company Members

Mungo Beaumont, Ellen Brammar, Emma Bright, Sophie Clay, Edward Cole, Marc Graham, Matthew May, Paul Smith and James Townsend.

Trustees

Amanda Smethurst (chair), Jack Heaton (vice-chair), Bellaray Bertrand-Webb, Hattie Callery, Tanya-Loretta Dee, Rachel Hogg, Cole Green, Harriet Johnson, Rozzy Knox, Charlotte Lines, Magda Moses, Amber Wiles and John R. Wilkinson.

Middle Child Mates

Middle Child's work is made possible by our pay what you can supporters' scheme, Middle Child Mates. Sign up today at middlechildtheatre.co.uk/donate

Middle Child is a company limited by guarantee (registered company number 09921306) and a charity (charity number 1188756).

Middle Child
42-43 High Street, Hull, HU1 1PS
+44(0)1482 221857
middlechildtheatre.co.uk

Biting Point

Sid Sagar is an actor, playwright and screenwriter from an Indian background. He grew up in England from the age of eight. He read History at the University of Bristol and trained with the Writers' Lab at Soho Theatre, the London Library Emerging Writers Programme, the Hampstead Theatre INSPIRE scheme, the Genesis Almeida New Playwrights Big Plays Programme, the Oxbelly Episodic Programme and the Channel 4 Screenwriting Course. As an actor, he won an Eastern Eye Award for Best Actor for his performance in Kenneth Lonergan's *The Starry Messenger* in the West End, as well as an AudioFile Earphones Award for his narration of Salman Rushdie's *Victory City*. Other credits include *Ballet Shoes* (National Theatre), *Cabaret* (West End) and *Slow Horses* (Apple TV+). As a writer, his work includes *Middle Men* (BBC Radio 4) and *John from Hemel* (BBC Radio 4). His first short film, *Baked Beans*, was produced by BFI NETWORK and was selected for festivals in the UK and internationally. He has been part of writers' rooms for Channel 4 and CBeebies and is developing a variety of projects for stage and screen. He is based in London.

SID SAGAR

Biting Point

faber

First published in 2025
by Faber and Faber Limited
The Bindery, 51 Hatton Garden, London EC1N 8HN
Typeset by Agnesi Text, Hadleigh, Suffolk
Printed in England by CPI Group (UK) Ltd, Croydon CR0 4YY

All rights reserved

© Sid Sagar, 2025

Sid Sagar is hereby identified as author
of this work in accordance with Section 77 of the
Copyright, Designs and Patents Act 1988

All rights whatsoever in this work, amateur or professional,
are strictly reserved. Applications for permission for any use
whatsoever including performance rights must be made in
advance, prior to any such proposed use, to 42 M&P Ltd, Palladium House,
7th Floor, 1–4 Argyll Street, London W1F 7TA

No performance may be given unless a licence
has first been obtained

This book is sold subject to the condition that it shall not,
by way of trade or otherwise, be lent, resold, hired out
or otherwise circulated without the publisher's prior consent
in any form of binding or cover other than that in which
it is published and without a similar condition including
this condition being imposed on the subsequent purchaser

A CIP record for this book is available from the British Library

ISBN 978–0–571–39882–9

Printed and bound in the UK on FSC® certified paper in line with our continuing
commitment to ethical business practices, sustainability and the environment.
For further information see faber.co.uk/environmental-policy

Our authorised representative in the EU for product safety is
Easy Access System Europe, Mustamäe tee 50, 10621 Tallinn, Estonia
gpsr.requests@easproject.com

9780571398829

1 2 4 6 8 10 9 7 5 3

Characters

John
male, thirties, White British

Anita
female, thirties, British South Asian

and lots of different recorded voices

Place and Time
Hull, England. Now.

Recorded Voices are communicated via the audience's headphones, and are shown here in **bold**.

This text went to print during rehearsals so may differ slightly from the version performed.

Biting Point was first performed at the Fruit Market multi-storey car park in Hull on 10 May 2025, before touring to car parks in Grimsby, Pocklington, Selby, Beverley, Redcar and Bridlington. The cast was as follows:

John Marc Graham
Anita Katie Singh

Voice Actors Sudha Bhuchar, Emma Bright, Jack Chamberlain, Sophie Clay, Emilio Encinoso-Gil, Amelia Grimes, Elle Ideson, Tony Jayawardena, Dan McGarry, Laura Meredith, Chris Pearson, Oliver Strong

Sensitivity Reader Jay Mitra
Director Paul Smith
Assistant Director Grace Waga Glevey
Dramaturg Matthew May
Designer Bethany Wells
Sound Designer Tom Smith
Movement Director Danielle Clements
Composer Kobby Taylor
Keys Vivek Santhosh
Lighting Designer Caitlin Clarke
Audience Experience Director Rachael Abbey
Artistic Collaborators Jay Mitra, Grace Waga Glevey
Producer Sarah Penney
Production Manager Danielle Harris
Company Stage Manager Shona Wright
Deputy Stage Manager Olivia Dudley
Technical Stage Manager Caitlin Clarke
Sound Engineer Jack Pellatt
BSL Interpreter (Hull) Dave Wycherley

With thanks to

Joan Iyiola, Polly Bennett, Alison Holder, Miles Sloman, Roberta Zuric, Bijan Sheibani and The Mono Box

Danny Kirrane

Kara Fitzpatrick

Davina Moss, Tessa Walker, Jennifer Davis, Roy Williams and the Hampstead Theatre

Dexter Flanders, Jessica Norman, Magda Bird, Martha Watson Allpress, Mary Clapp, Nancy Netherwood, Nic McQuillan, Nicola May-Taylor, Patrick Swain, Phoebe Frances Brown and Sarah Power

Paul Keating, Ian Drysdale, Stuart Thompson, Claire Price, Emily Barber and Sudha Bhuchar

Marc Graham, Dan McGarry, Sophie Clay, Laura Meredith and Manjinder Virk

Dinah Wood and Lily Levinson

Daniel Lapaine

Harrison Davies and Charlotte Goffin

Paul Smith, Matthew May and Middle Child

Georgia Green

Mum, Papa and Diya

BITING POINT

1

John is in a cheap suit, tie loose, headphones on, nodding along to music, holding a bundle of important-looking documents, gazing at the view.

When it feels right, he notices the audience, takes his headphones off and addresses them directly.

John You need to know that when that Nissan Micra clipped my bumper on the Wingfield Farm roundabout, just after the junction with the A15

We stopped
 And I was pissed off because now I'd be late
 And I get paid for the time that I'm there and lateness doesn't help that one bit.

You need to know that

You need to know that I've always been anxious. That I've always struggled to control those anxieties. That I wasn't born anxious but maybe, just maybe, my mum knew exactly what world I was entering into and that her own worries wormed their way into me. Because these things are linked, aren't they? You don't drink or smoke when a human's growing inside you but you can't help it when the man you married because he was initially a charmer with a heart of gold is causing you all sorts of upset. And I think those worries made it to me. Now I'm no scientist, hate science, think it's dull as fuck, but it doesn't take a rocket scientist to know that science is significant. And maybe I'd have a better grasp of nature and nurture if my school wasn't shit and my teachers gave a shit and I didn't

Fall
 Off the rails

Age ten, I beat someone up. Well, couple of punches and a kick but it did the trick. I had to walk the long way home. Around this field of pitches and pavilions and private school money. I mean what the fuck is a pavilion? I certainly didn't know but the boys in the blue blazers certainly did. They played and played and played and I always had to walk the long way home. And this boy in a blue blazer he called me a chav. And I don't know why. Well, I do know why. But I don't know what that really means. But I do know that it felt fucking good to see him in the mud with blood on his lip and his nose and his eyes filled with fear. And when my foot connected with his side . . . Jesus Christ. He gasped and bulged and . . . Jesus Christ. It was a shame really because it seemed to prove that although I didn't live in a council house I was very much capable of some pretty explicit violence.

You need to tell them that against all odds I got to twenty-five with a degree and a job

And I was doing okay.

2

Anita enters in a rush, wearing a dressing gown and holding a coffee.
  She slows herself down. She closes her eyes. She puts a finger to her nose, closes a nostril, breathes in, then out, then does the same to the other nostril. A breathing exercise designed to be calming and meditative . . . Then her eyes snap open, wide.

Anita If all the yoga malarkey actually worked, why am I still so bloody wired? Fuck it. It's presentation day. There's a gig to clinch. A client that's so nearly mine and I do really need this contract because . . . well, I'm not quite meeting those targets so the commission is drying up and you know how the story goes. So, instead, let's focus on this one. Let's get Anita through and seal the bloody deal! No questions at this time, please and thank you, just keep staring ahead, that's right, no smiling allowed, not even a sly nervous grin to your shy nervous mate who doesn't quite know why you've dragged them here.

I mean, look, no one grins in a meeting about expanding a property portfolio and changing the managing agent of a block in disrepair, it's not really giving *Live at the Apollo* vibes, but I guess that's the world of work and adulting and Jesus Christ, Anita! Get it together, love. And maybe one day remember to replace those Nespresso pods in the kitchen because another dawn-breaker of instant coffee in a KeepCup and your bowels will wreak havoc at the least opportune of moments.

She takes a sip from her coffee. She grimaces.

God, that's rank. Like warm tar.

She tips the cup upside down, chucking coffee dregs onto the ground.

Genuinely thought I'd seen a drain there. Is that ... am I littering? Is coffee tipping in a public place a bit like ... fly tipping? No matter, I'll mop up, goddess in the kitchen me, always tidying up after others, always making things gleam and shine in time for someone else to keep their shoes on and bring in the mud and dust and shit of the outside world. No matter, no worries, I'll clean up later, I'm just OCD is all, that must be it, I need to take a chill pill!

She's distracted by the coffee puddle on the ground.

But you should know, actually, that ...

You need to know that there's a life out there I might have lived had I turned the indicator on in time, left some room for manoeuvres, anticipated what was ahead and around the corner

    Looked out and up and over
    Looked through the mirror, properly tried, strained, if I'd realised it wasn't a reflection but actually, maybe, just a very misleading window

Dirty, grubby, in need of a dash of Flash or Viakal or maybe just your bog-standard anti-bac wipes, own brand will do

Because through that window there's another version of me
    Gazing into a future filled with the doors of opportunity
    Stardom maybe
    Can you imagine?

Instead, though, I kept seeing bloody mirrors
    Like one of those creepy houses at a funfair
    Faces staring back at me
    Mainly mine
    I couldn't stop looking
    Call me vain, fine
    But I couldn't stop being bothered
    I didn't like what I could I see
    I couldn't stop looking
    And sometimes that look would get me into trouble.

The sounds of a busy kitchen, pots and pans, oil and meat sizzling.

Anita's Dad What's wrong, *bachcha*?

Anita's Mum She's just sulking. Leave her.

Anita's Dad Sulking? Why?

Anita's Mum She won't tell me anything.

Anita's Dad We all get the grumpy grumps sometimes. School was okay?

Anita's Mum I've made the kebabs you like, Anita, there's *raita* in the fridge, I'll put this *naan* in the oven and someone needs to set the table –

Anita's Dad I'll do it. I'm doing it.

Anita's Mum Wait! Stop. Those aren't dry. Look!

Anita's Dad What are you saying? They're dry. It's dry.

Anita's Mum Stop, for God's sake, always making things worse –

Anita's Dad They're dry, *yaar*.

Anita's Mum Look down! Look at the splashes! I wipe the floor God knows how many times and you drag these plates and bowls making puddles when I've told you –

Anita's Dad Fine. Do it yourself.

Anita's Mum Water everywhere when I tell you every time that these things need to be left to dry, I tell you every time and still –

A door slams in the distance.

Stupid man. Anita, will you –

Anita Can I get laser?

Anita's Mum What?

Anita Laser. On my . . . to get rid of this . . . all this.

Anita's Mum No. You don't need it.

Anita I do.

Anita's Mum Just use the thread.

Anita It doesn't work.

Anita's Mum It's a tradition from ancient times, darling, I think it does –

Anita It doesn't. And my stupid DNA means I end up with a tash and looking like some . . . some stupid brown detective.

Meat sizzles. A smoke alarm starts beeping.

Anita's Mum Oh for crying out – (*Calling to Anita's dad.*) Wave the towel in front of the thing! Did you hear me? Wave it! (*To Anita.*) The table, Anita. Start setting. The kebabs burn and then the whole dinner is ruined.

Anita Kebab.

The smoke alarm turns off.

It's kebab.

Anita's Mum What?

Anita Not 'kebaaab'. Just say it normally, Mum, for fuck's sake.

Pause.

It's presentation day and my mind's wandering, playing tricks, running rings around me and I've not even had a chance to look through my notes yet, it's a bit of a nightmare but busy is good, it's good to be busy, it keeps you going, keeps you on, keep on keeping on, I like that phrase, it's active, it's forward, and there's nothing I like more than a bit of forward momentum. Because it's not all doom and gloom, it's not all buried in our past, there's only so many times you can sit on your arse and tear up and blame it on your parents, what they did and didn't do, how they loved and hated, how they triumphed and catastrophically failed, there's only so many minutes in the day to keep looking back. That's history, isn't it? And I was never really that into it at school or college, wars and conflict and consequence are all very relevant, of course, but there came a time when I'd be looking through those textbooks with hairy kings and chubby queens and all the bloody *violence* and, well, blood that seemed to sum up humanity's best efforts from the last one thousand years, and that sort of thing keeps me from moving on, it stops the forward momentum, it drags me into reverse without sight of the rear-view mirror, it takes my mind away from presentations and appraisals and stakeholders and I could swear it's determined to ruin it all –

The Ex Do you want kids then?

The sounds of a warm, buzzy pub.

Sorry. Bit intense. I, uh, I just –

Anita No, no, you're fine. I like a bit of directness.

The Ex Yeah?

Anita Makes a change from the everyday, y'know? All the fake politeness and tight smiles and –

The Ex Who have *you* been hanging around with?

Anita No one, really. I just . . . I guess sometimes I feel like –

The Ex People don't say what they really think. Or believe?

Anita Yeah. Yeah, exactly.

The Ex I know what you mean.

Anita It's just . . . I'm not like a therapist or something, I'm not a *savant* –

The Ex What's that?

Anita Oh. Fancy word for like . . . a genius, I think?

The Ex Right. Should have just said that then.

Pause.

I'm joking. Little callback to being *direct* . . . Jesus. Sorry. I'm nervous, I think. Sorry.

Anita Nervous? Why?

The Ex Well. Why d'you think?

Anita smiles.

Anita What did Lauren tell you about me, then?

The Ex Nothing. I just . . . Have I said too much?

Anita No. It's funny, that's all. That you're nervous. It's sweet.

Pause.

I wondered what Lauren might have said about me. Law unto herself, that one. I shouldn't think about it, really, it's none of my business, and besides if you're here, then that's surely a sign that she hasn't said anything particularly concerning. Not that she would have done, I love her to bits. I mean . . . what's there to say? I'm in my mid-twenties, I grew up in Grimsby, my freezer's full of food that my mum still cooks for me like I'm some incapable child, I think I might be happy in my job but I'm also wondering if I wasted several years doing a degree that doesn't mean anything. And I don't seem to have much luck when it comes to, y'know . . .

The Ex Relationships?

Anita Bingo.

The Ex Well. You can only try. Fail better. Fail upwards?

Anita If you're a bloke, maybe.

The Ex Oops. Walked into that one.

Pause.

You didn't answer my question.

Anita Oh. Sorry. What did –

The Ex Kids. D'you think . . . like, how d'you feel about kids?

3

A slightly groggy John appears, in trackies, T-shirt and hi-vis vest. Maybe the sounds of birdsong and early morning.

VO Six a.m. Eight hours and thirty minutes before John approaches the Wingfield Farm roundabout.

John Shit. Shower. I'll shave tomorrow. This shadow's all right actually. Something mysterious about it.

It's dawn. Pre-dawn, really. Too early.

Head's pounding, slightly. Should have known better. One of the many things I've not known until it's a bit late.

Could smash a Lucozade right now but the fridge is big and empty. Been meaning to do a big shop but that'll have to wait. Maybe grab some yellow stickers from the staff shop. It's the same products as what they have in the stores but it might have been returned, you see. Maybe the packaging was dented or it was about to be chucked or . . . boring, John. Fuck me.

So it's dawn. Pre-dawn, really. Lids are heavy.

Roads at this time are a godsend, though. Nothing better than springing into summer, window three-quarters down, endless green lights and shifting from third to fourth.

Still in a mood, though. Still wondering about the things that I could have said and the things I wish I didn't. But that's what radios are for, I guess.

John turns the radio on.

Radio We have Kelly from Sheffield on the line!

Kelly Morning, you lot!

Radio Go on then, Kelly, couple of quick-fire ones for ya before we get our Dua Lipa fix. Cats or dogs, Kelly?

Kelly Oh, I dunno, I'm more of a cat person I think? But I do really like dogs sometimes.

John Jesus Christ.

Radio How about holidays, Kelly? Week by the pool or city break?

Kelly It's gotta be Prosecco o'clock on the sun-lounger!

Radio Love that, Kelly!

John It's all right. There's always –

He changes the station.

Radio Minister, how do you respond to that allegation?

Minister Well, it's all very well blaming the government, but what solutions are they offering? Have the Shadow Cabinet proposed any viable alternative beyond simplistic –

John Fuck off.

He changes the station again. This time it's mellow, soothing.

Seems simple, sometimes. Wonder if I should have gone in for that. A career in the corridors of power. Nice suits and juicy expenses and maybe a vague feeling of doing . . . something.

I know this route so well that my mind can wander. Safely, of course.

Dunno why, but it keeps going to school. Leaky memories of a strange conversation with a thin-faced woman and her unpleasant smile. Probation officer, she said. That's what my form suggested. That would be the career best suited to my skills and interests in people and law and making some kind of change. There was always volunteering, too. Or the council. Sorting out bins. Fences. But instead –

4

Harsh, grating sounds of vans and lorries reversing. Tannoy and alarms in the distance as John shows a trainee, Leanne, how to conduct a van check.

Leanne It's so early, isn't it?

John Yeah. I suppose so.

VO Six forty a.m. Seven hours and fifty minutes before John approaches the Wingfield Farm roundabout.

Leanne Can't remember the last time I was up this early. Sort of feels like we're up earlier than everyone else? Which I guess we sort of are.

John Leanne's a trainee. And I've been gifted the opportunity to show her the ropes, introduce her to the vans, make sure she feels safe and secure for the glamorous journey ahead. But it's tricky with the trainees because they get in ahead of you with words of wisdom like –

Leanne Oh cool, it's already loaded.

John Yeah. That's a different job. We're drivers. There are pickers. And there are loaders. The pickers pick. The loaders . . . load.

Leanne I think remember. From the training.

John Bright spark, this one. She'll probably be a line manager in six months. If she doesn't do a runner like the rest of the kids with hopes and dreams –

Leanne Shit pickers.

John What?

Leanne That's what they call the loaders, right? 'Shit pickers'. Sorry, maybe I shouldn't have said anything. Just trying to get in with the banter –

John Leanne.

Leanne Sorry.

John No, it's all right, I don't mean to interrupt, I just . . . I need to show you these van checks so I can get out on the road.

Leanne Right. Go for it.

John It's just I'm slightly up against it. That's all.

Pause.

Feeling bad now, not *bad*, just a bit annoyed, not even at Leanne, just the bloody situation. Not my fault I've got no time to train a trainee and not Leanne's fault she's been lumped with me, but then again, what's the point in getting someone like her on board for a few weeks when all she's really interested in is that sweet sterling in her bank account so she can spend it on bloody . . . ASOS? Or whatever it is these days. Jesus. I sound like my dad.

Leanne You all right, John?

John Yep. So, you've got your standard checks. Like you'd do for any . . . any vehicle, really. Treat it like you're hiring a car on your holidays or whatever. Take a video, if you want. Of the condition. Probably best to do that, actually. Some of the drivers leave them in a state. So, yeah. Mirrors, obviously. Lights. You obviously can't see your back lights, the reversing lights, or your indicators, so you need to flag someone down before setting off and just ask them to help you out. You can return the favour at another point. Another shift or whatever.

Pause.

Yeah, I've definitely lost her, so maybe this is a moment for some lightness, bit of warmth, let that banter loose, so I say, Leanne?

Leanne Yeah?

John Do us a favour. Funny noise coming from the bonnet. Could you lean in?

Leanne Lean in?

John Yeah. Could you just lean in slightly and see if you hear it as well?

Leanne Um . . . I can't hear anything? Maybe it's –

John beeps the van horn.

Fuck me! Jesus Christ.

John Sorry I was just – that's a, that was a –

Leanne Ow. It's just . . . I had an ear infection last week and I'm still on antibiotics and that really –

John Sorry. Sorry, Leanne. I was joking around. Bit of a competition between the drivers here and anyway – fucking hell, John, what was the point in that? – anyway there's this plug which charges the fridge and freezer. You have to remember to unplug it, which seems like a daft thing to say but it's easy to forget, especially if you're in a rush –

Leanne Like a Tesla?

John You what?

Leanne Like a plug for an electric car?

John Um. No. It's for the freezer. And the fridge.

Leanne I'm *obsessed*.

John With what? Fridges?

Leanne Electric cars. And, like, all the technology that you need to use them? I was studying this unit last year about sustainability . . .

She fades away as John continues.

John And she's off. I mean, I've heard it all before, I've heard a lot worse, said a lot worse, think a lot, think a tonne, think a whole 2.5 tonnes, that's the size of these vans with their chargers and their freezers. I look at someone like Leanne with her wide eyes and hair in a bun and that crisp crisp hi-vis jacket and I think, actually, it doesn't suit her, none of this suits her, she's not meant for here, she's designed for something else. And that tick-tock knocking in my chest in my tummy in my head, still pounding, it's getting thick and heavy now instead of the spiky spark it was when the alarm went off, but that tick-tocking is coming for me again, but it's not like school, or uni, when it was fainter, distant, when I still had my hands on the second hand, when I could reset it on the fly, now it's faster, stronger, stronger than I am that's for sure, bigger than me with my five feet and eleven inches and this naughty paunch around my waist and the T-shirt that's been washed so many times the colour's come off and I think I'm running out of time –

Leanne Can you ever, like, go out?

John What, like –

Leanne *Out* out?

John Clubbing?

Leanne Yeah. Like. Get pissed. And stuff. If you're always working this early.

John I'm usually on later shifts. Two till ten. Not six till two. So yeah. I can go out.

The distant thrum of a nightclub. Echoey, raucous laughter.

I forgot I was on early actually. Today. Thought I was on my usual rota.

Katie Men and their mums, eh?

The music fades away.

John I forgot. So . . . yeah. I went out.

Leanne What? Last night?

John Yeah.

Leanne Fair play. You must be knackered.

John Am a bit, yeah.

Pause.

I didn't . . . you know . . .

Leanne What?

John Doesn't matter.

Pause.

Don't forget to unplug the charger. Or they'll dock the repairs from your wages. All right?

5

John, in the van, on the road.

VO Seven thirty-five a.m. Six hours and fifty-five minutes before John approaches the Wingfield Farm roundabout.

John This drop is all over the place. I said that to him, to Trev, upstairs, he's covering rotas, sorts out the drops using tech or something, he's always in the office, decent lad, bit annoying, could do with shaking up the diet, can't be good for your insides living off Greggs and Orangina. I said that to him – about the drops, I mean, not the diet – and he just goes –

Trev It's lemon squeezy, mate.

John But it's not, I said, it's mental. It's all over the place, Trev. I –

Trev Shouldn't be saying things like 'mental', John. There's new guidance been issued, you should have got an email, it's about appropriate language in the workplace and don't look at me like that, pal, I don't make the rules –

John Right, I said, sure, but look – it's Hessle, Swanland, Willerby, Hessle, Spring Back, Vicky Dock, back out to Anlaby, but there's roadworks on the A63 so –

Trev Looks worse than it is, mate. For all that pisses me off about the technology, in her defence, Mrs Google Maps really does know her way around the postcodes of Hull and the East Riding . . .

He fades away as John continues.

John The talk just slows you down. So I grab a coffee from the machine in the break room, card reader's broken, course it is, no change, fuck it, down to the yard, head still pounding, not drinking enough water, that must be it, so I get away with the final checks, bit half-arsed tell you the truth, the only one really worth doing is the horn because it's quite funny making the other drivers shit themselves, bloody trainees though, Leanne was it? She needs to lighten up, it's a generational thing, sound like my dad again, Jesus, I'm about to slam the door and start the engine and shut myself away from the shit, I'm about to do it, I'm about to get into freedom, I can feel it, it's where I think I might belong, in a firm-cushioned seat raised above the ground with my hand on the gear and a foot on the clutch and letting your left rise as the right pushes down and you get to that point where the world's in front but I'm still above it, only slightly, a vantage point, a viewing gallery, I'm nearly there but –

Trev You've not unplugged the EV charger, John.

John Shit. Sorry. Sorry, Trev. I was –

Trev But they are quite dear, John. The chargers. You've got to unplug them before heading off. If I had a penny every time a driver destroyed an EV charger . . . Well,

let's just say I wouldn't be up before dawn covering Tina's maternity leave!

John Trev used to be a driver but he's risen through the ranks and won't let anyone forget it. His style of management is a middling five-minute set in a struggling club in a former industrial town, followed by a sudden twist of the administrative knife, right in your emotional spine, right where it hurts –

Trev Funny things, spreadsheets. Like a less stimulating Candy Crush.

John Foot hovering on gas. But they record us, you see, they analyse every move, every gear shift, every emergency stop, every time you're running out of time, so you think fuck it I can make it through that orange before it turns red, so you step on it, you put your foot to the floor in a van that's not built for it, and it's people like Trev who know you're accelerating at an unhealthy rate on a consistent basis, and it's people like Trev who say things like –

Trev There's a lot of red, John.

John You what?

Trev You're familiar with this spreadsheet, of course? Green, you're meeting expectations, amber could do with improvement, red is . . . Tell me if I'm missing something, John, but all this red, for me, quite clearly suggests your approach to driving these vans is . . .

John What?

Trev A little off. To be frank.

John My drops today are all over the place. It's properly fucked. I don't say that to him, not again anyway, I don't give Trev another reason to think that I'm only at work so I can get home as quickly as possible, but there's something about how he said –

Trev To be frank.

John And sitting in a queue, trying to get out of North Ferriby, fucking roadworks, temporary lights system and a whole lane is closed and you have to wait at least seven minutes before your turn comes round again, but the dickhead in front is taking his time and slowing down when it's still bloody *green*, for fuck's sake, I understand safety, safety first of course, but it's not very safe for the beating in my mind, for the tapping in my fingers, to run so fucking late, and it's because it's not dawn anymore, is it? It's basically rush hour in Hull now, but it's less frolics with Jackie Chan and Chris Tucker, more lasses with fake tan and lorries driven by some chunky fuckers, and I remember a man I used to know.

He was called Frank. I've always liked that name. I trust it.

I always liked our conversations.

6

CRASH. Distant traffic.

John You need to know that against all odds I got to twenty-nine
    And I was doing okay
    The job was providing with good chances of progression
    I played football on a Sunday and I sometimes went to the pub
    And realised I could love
    I could love and love and love and love
    And I had a job
    And I volunteered
    I volunteered
    I gave time to others and it reminded me of pain
    And I think I was better for it

You need to tell them that I have done good things
  And that I will do so again
  You need to tell them that
  That I've worked with the homeless
  That I rang a man named Frank, once a week, for fifteen minutes, for a year, to offer him companionship
  And we chatted about everything, including but not limited to
  Ballroom dancing and Bolton Wanderers
  Golden retrievers and the Golden Gate Bridge
  And the things we missed

But when that Nissan Micra clipped my bumper on the Wingfield Farm roundabout, just after the junction with the A15
  I saw red

The traffic lights up ahead were green then orange
  I saw red

The leaves on the dirty trees by the side of that busy road were autumnal and orange
  I could only see red

And then I saw her.

7

A kettle boils as Anita enters, smartly dressed in work clothes, lanyard around her neck.

VO Six fifteen a.m. Eight hours and fifteen minutes before Anita approaches the Wingfield Farm roundabout.

Anita I dream of the day when it doesn't feel like every moment before leaving the house is a slight panic-in-your-chest-have-I-forgotten-something-maybe-everything series of utter shitshows. I dream of those days and try and brand them into my actual dreams, when my head hits the pillow and I'm out for the count because the day before has turned into a nightmare. And look, it's usually not that bad, maybe I'm exaggerating, I'm known for exaggerating, everyone says so, they think it's funny and I did too for a bit until I realised that a lot of stories I told would immediately be followed by little looks and knowing glances and sometimes I just feel like grabbing one of the anti-allergy pillows from Maya's room and screaming

I AM NOT EXAGGERATING

THIS IS NOT HYPERBOLE

THIS IS MY FUCKING TRUTH

Or something less . . . mental. I dunno.

Anyway, Anita, fix up, look sharp, there are meetings to make and files to file and contractors to contract and clients to smile at and tenants to avoid and landlords to thrill and Maya's away, thank God, not thank God like that – I love her, obviously, she's my bloody daughter, she's heaven on earth, she's an angel in the guise of tantrums and an unnerving addiction to *Bluey* – but she's been in Center Parcs with her dad for three days now and I miss her dearly, I miss her like a bit of my heart is stuck in the week before. Him less so, decent bloke, used to be funny, shouldn't have married so soon because we were young and confused and once we realised we should talk stuff out the stuff that came out was pretty . . . horrible, really.

So Maya's in Center Parcs with her dad but they're back tonight and then it's my turn but in the dawn of today, in the pre-dawn really, the world asleep but my mind doing somersaults like an Olympian on their last legs, in the dawn of today it hits me that all the things I was supposed to have done while I had time to myself have just . . . not. And I can't even blame him for that. That's on me. Fuck's sake, Anita.

So there are still emails and catch-ups and appraisals and a bloody site visit – can't stand a site visit, the sight of them in the iCal and shivers visit my spine – I know, I'm exaggerating, but I'm just trying to make a point. The annual leave clock is ticking and as of four fifty-six p.m. the emails will bounce back and I'll be bouncing forward into a week of maybe reading that book about the pensioner detectives and Maya needing new shoes and a box set would be nice, something Scandi, something *noir*, and then inventing new lunches for my little girl while trying not to destroy the kitchen and maybe a trip to the coast and all the glorious fun that comes with checking your weather app four hundred times, hoping for the best, landing on a beach off the North Sea and trying to stop Maya from getting hypothermia.

VO Eight thirty a.m. Six hours before Anita approaches the Wingfield Farm roundabout.

Anita No space in the car park even though they said there would be. Sign coming in says you get a fifteen-minute grace period before the cameras log it in the system and the system sees you leave sixteen minutes later and there'll be a letter coming through, mark my words, there'll be a bloody letter. There's always a letter, a bill, a notice, a statement of intent, there'll always be something to keep you from properly breathing so when you somehow manage to see an actual living human doctor in real life, a GP in HD and 3D and they glance up from their monitor, ready to bat away another time waster, and they look at you with a heavy frown and they say –

GP Are you experiencing any stress at the moment?

Pause.

Anita Stress?

GP Do you think there's anything which might be causing a state of worry or mental tension?

Anita How long have you got?

GP Obviously, we all experience stress to some degree. But too much stress can affect our mood, our body, our relationships.

Anita Right.

GP In some cases, leading to a kind of burnout.

Pause.

Here's a leaflet with some useful next steps.

Anita Thanks.

GP Would you like a referral for CBT?

Anita CBT?

GP Cognitive behavioural therapy. It's –

Anita I know what it is. I've tried it before.

So instead I collect a repeat prescription, they've raised the prices again and no yes I do pay thank you very much, another bulging packet of creams and sprays and lotions and potions to deal with this forever feeling of itchiness and redness and rawness and affliction that keeps me from starting the day without checking if my skin's peeling off. Too much information? Maya loves saying that. TMI, Mummy! Yucky yucky, and to be fair to her, it is a bit.

It starts in childhood, the itching in the elbows, behind the knees, and as you grow it grows with you, an unwanted accessory, I'd rather a third nipple, a mole on my bum, a twitch in my hips or something, not fucking eczema. Endless, endless, skin-crawling, skin-tweezing, skin-ruining. Waking up with an itch, if it's wet keep it dry, if it's dry it needs moisture, Anita, lathering myself through the day like some shit spa in any spare moment between Maya and work and a meeting about a meeting and dashing into the loos and getting in front of the mirror, covering up, always

bloody covering up, might as well wear a mask at this rate
I'm so conscious of meeting a client and them looking at my
crusty eyelids or peeling neck and thinking actually maybe
it's better to take my business elsewhere, maybe I'll just pay
the same commission down the road with that gorgeous
blonde girl with the fair, hairless skin and the blue blue eyes
and her vanilla office where everything looks and smells
clean but instead they're looking at me, and probably I've
not wiped it in enough, I tend to do that, start moisturising
and then forget because something's got my attention
and needs it more than the thin skin under my eyes, or
the cracked bits at the bottom of my scalp, and I always
follow their gaze, maybe it's harmless, maybe they're just
wandering as we all wander, but I can't help but wonder if
they're looking at me and feeling ever so slightly repulsed.
What? What the fuck is it? I feel like saying it out loud, to
their face, wonder what their face would look like if I did,
if I had the balls to cut through the shit and say what I
finally mean, say it to their face, ask them, demand them to
come clean with me, to fully disclose without any exclusions
or terms and conditions, just tell me what the fucking
problem is –

Plumber It's the plumbing.

Anita You what?

Plumber Whoever did it when the flats were first built, well, they've royally messed up.

Anita How so?

Plumber Where d'you want me to begin? You'd never install a water tank for shared usage the way they have. It's no wonder you've got residents causing a fuss.

Anita Okay. So –

Plumber It's typical of these new builds. Crap builds, more like. They get the contract then chuck 'em up in no time, no due diligence, surveyors are skimming off the developer so they'll *forget* to note down basic omissions. Same old story. See, what you learn, love, when you've been in this game for as long as I have . . .

He fades away as Anita continues.

Anita Has a plumber ever given anyone good news? Have they ever turned up and said, oh, wow, I realise the flush hasn't been working but whoever was here before did a smashing job with the tiles! And don't worry about the call-out charge, happy to waive it on this occasion given your loyalty and the fact that our hourly rate was spent gathering mysterious supplies from a shop we won't call Amazon and no worries we accept cheques, pay us in thirty days, pay us never, no point really, seeing as we've just increased our fees at 10 per cent above RPI for no good reason. I wonder as he bangs on, listing in full and impossible detail the various faults caused by someone else, it's always someone else, it's never their guy, it's never their mate, it's another bloke whose screwed up further down the line, and when I get back to the office I'll let them know, we'll get the report back and the invoice and I'll make a cup of tea. God, I could do with a cuppa right now, an air-conditioned office with a milk no sugar, desktop facing away from the others, maybe headphones on to show everyone that they should at all costs avoid talking to me and definitely put it in an email –

Resident Are you from the company? Are you the property manager?

Anita Shit. I was about to get in the car but I've still got my lanyard on and it's fairly obvious at this point that yes, yes I am, I'm a senior property manager I'm just on a site visit actually and a little pushed for time, would you mind –

Resident Months I've been trying to get in touch with you lot! Maybe you'd prefer me heading into town, knocking on the door, having a proper word?

Anita Sorry, what's . . . I'm a little –

Resident You don't respond to emails. You tell me you'll call back. Meanwhile I get my bills for the maintenance on the month every month and they're going up faster than Usain Bolt round a running track and what am I getting in return, eh?

Anita Look. I can see you're frustrated but it really is best to get in touch with the team in the office, like I said I'm a senior property manager but this site is usually looked after by my colleague and I'm just covering their leave, so it would be best –

Resident I can't sell! I can't bloody sell!

Anita What do you –

Resident Estate agents come round, take one look at the building, then ask me about the company, about you lot, about how much I'm paying, how much it's going up, the ground rent and all, the fucking cash I throw down the drain because this system is bent, they tell me no buyer would touch this place with a bargepole –

Anita Look, I can see you're angry –

Resident Trust me, pet, you'll know when I'm angry. Time wasters. Bunch of fucking thieves.

Anita And he goes. And I get in the car. Into my Nissan Micra. Doors shut, locks down, radio on –

She turns the radio on.

Radio So if you've got an embarrassing name we want to hear it! If you've just tuned in, you missed a hilarious chat with Sophie Dickie in Lincoln, there was also Tom Bellenden in Scunthorpe –

Anita Radio off and silence.

And I idle.

Just idle.

And then I'm driving on autopilot like I'm up in the sky,
the captain of clouds, nothing but blue and sun, windows
up even though it's too warm for this time of year, it's
the climate, it's changing, it keeps Maya awake, she loves
animals, loves nature, loves the outdoors but in the summer
she can't sleep, it's too warm in here Mummy please can
I come in with you

And I drive.

The office is back in town and everything's moving quite
slowly today but my mind is racing, hundred miles an hour
it's going, it's Lewis Hamilton on a mad one, I can't stop it
even though the leaflets say it's best to take some breaths,
I'm so close to a bit of a break and I want to see Maya,
I want to glance at her in the mirror, to see me and a bit of
him staring back with thoughts on the ceiling and that grin
on her face, cheeky monkey, she's my dream, she's my queen,
and the traffic is moving and there are so many hotels in this
city and I never really noticed that before, there are loads,
dotted off this main road as you head back into town, and
there's a shopping centre and a big Tesco, an all-you-can-
eat Chinese which is always empty and some places are
boarded up, hoping for better days, some are clinging on to
the past, how are there so many gyms in this city, who needs
all these gyms, maybe that might help my skin, fat chance,
stumbling on a treadmill and melting on a CrossFit and
changing my diet and giving up dairy and drinking more
water and getting more fibre and only white meat and river
fish, salmon doesn't count, Anita, then it's the station flying
by and then it's lights up ahead and it's the cheap blue sign
of Hull's Royal Hotel

They gathered here
Sun shining, police in hi-vis, flags and faces

They gathered –

Driver Fucking move, man!

Traffic and distant horn beeping.

Anita I move. Just manage to sneak out of the yellow box. Glance in the mirror at the bearded red face behind me, hands in the air, inflamed by the situation, aggrieved by the delay, ripe and ready to burst by the looks of things when, back down there, that hotel on Ferensway, they tried to burn it down.

Sun shining, police in hi-vis, flags and faces

I move.

8

The hiss and steam of an espresso machine.

John Feeling more human after a coffee. Nausea's abated, sitting down for a bit, giving me a chance to clear my head.

VO Ten twenty a.m. Four hours and ten minutes before John approaches the Wingfield Farm roundabout.

John I get a thirty-minute break on shift but you have to log it on the device, on the device thingy, it's like a satnav and schedule and nightmare rolled into one, can put it on your wrist like a big ugly watch, usually I peg it for a coffee, speed onto a double yellow, hazards on, quick slash, and only log it on the device thingy once the coffee's come because sometimes these posh places take the piss. No urgency. I'm wearing hi-vis, for fuck's sake, I'm not sitting around with the Bible or playing cards with my nanna, I've got places to be, time is literally money for me, but the twelve-year-old barista can't remember what milk it was so I remind them it's normal and they say –

Barista Normal?

John Normal. Yeah. Cow.

Barista Oh. Right. I think this one's –

John I'll have it. Whatever. It's fine, honestly, I –

Barista It's coconut.

John You what?

Barista I made it with coconut? Do you want me to –

John No. It's fine. So I have a coconut coffee in the end and it does the job, sort of, but now that I'm back in the van and the coffee is drunk and the muffin is munched it's suddenly back again. The feeling. It's more than a hangover, this.

Outside, minutes ticking down on the break timer, there's an actual timer, honest to God, makes you feel like you're carrying a bomb and would it be the worst thing to just trust a driver to take a break without monitoring me like I'm on fucking parole, I'm delivering bog roll and Babybels, I'm not on day release, and this hangover that's not a hangover but is definitely related to an overindulgence is seeding its way from the pits of my tummy through the knots of my chest and clawing at me up top, it's in my head again, there are thoughts I'm avoiding and regretting and I can't quite make sense of them. Or I can, but I don't want to.

Minutes to go now but I'm not ready and that coconut is rank actually, who'd choose that over cow or oat or even bloody almond if you're really scraping the barrel and it's too warm, but I can't take off the vest, or I can, but then some customers get sketchy if they think you're just some random bloke but what does this hi-vis really do for me, what does it actually *do* for me, like properly, apart from marking me out as someone to avoid, someone highly invisible to the patterns and structures of the day and its processes, I'm not making people tick and I'm not part of the ways in which this world works. I look them in the eye sometimes, I dare them to think of me what they no doubt will when they see this vest and the sweat on my forehead and the black under my nails and I know what's going on in their heads but mark my words they don't know what's going on in mine.

Seagulls, wind, the sounds of the marina.

I'm on a double yellow but I peg it over that bridge from Prinny Quay, traffic down below, snail's pace, tooting horns, that'll be me again in a minute for fuck's sake but for now it's down the ramp and looking out away from grey and roads and fuming air and it's the marina, Jesus, there's a bloody marina in this city, it's properly lush, don't know a thing about boats but I sometimes see them lined up all white and shiny with funny names and I reckon I'd be a good sailor, what I wouldn't give for a week on a yacht in the Med with a lager in hand and not a care in the world and just knowing that I was in this world but I could also get away from it, and I need to get away, I need a break, I do, I think I might book a holiday, though even saying that out loud suddenly makes me terrified of the beating throbbing isolation of it all, that's what they say, isn't it, philosophers and writers and fancy professors, they say you never feel lonelier then when you're in a city surrounded by the rest of life, so what I wouldn't give for one of these boats and the Humber just beyond inviting me, telling me it's all maybe possible. It's maybe my way out. Because when I look back up and the beeping starts on the device, the bloody device thingy, my break is done, my thirty minutes have disappeared into thin air, the time I'll never get back and I've spent it looking at boats I'll never sail and drinking coconuts like some puppy in a cartoon and it's back out to Swanland for me, that's the far west of the city, where there's happy families with mortgages paid and two cars in the drive that need their sourdough starter but actually my heart is pulling me east, to a home, not *my* home though I guess that is home when I think about it, but further than that, up Holderness Road, keep going and I'll get to that hospice and I'll get to Mum and I might bring her back even though it's not possible but imagine if it was though, imagine if I could, they say it's best to visit as and when but they know it's difficult, they say they understand, and it's not just work even though I always say it's work, it's often work but it's usually because I don't know what to say and they say I should call ahead but something's telling me it's gonna be them calling me, and they say I'm bringing the gift of my presence, it says it online and in the leaflets and I've read those words over and over and over again and they say the reticence is natural they say it's all fine and they say I should try and talk about where it's coming from maybe, and I feel like shouting, screaming, going into that reception and telling them

DON'T YOU FUCKING UNDERSTAND?

That's what I'd say.

I'd say

I'd say it's my mum

It's my mum

And I wish it was my dad.

9

The following is told entirely through headphones.

VO Eleven a.m. Three and a half hours before John approaches the Wingfield Farm roundabout. And around twenty-four years since he pretended to be asleep in the back of his dad's car.

John's Dad I wish he'd speak to the others.

John's Mum I thought he did.

John's Dad Not properly.

John's Mum He was tired.

John's Dad He's a worrier.

John's Mum Rob, please.

John's Dad What?

John's Mum The brakes, Rob. The brakes. Makes me feel sick.

John's Dad Shouldn't have had so much wine.

John's Mum Had to have something to get me through that! Their whole house was filled floor to ceiling with . . . boring people.

John's Dad You wouldn't know a decent person if they slapped you in the face.

John's Mum Watch it.

John's Dad It's true. And don't think Gary and Sandra can't tell.

John's Mum I don't care what Gary and Sandra think.

John's Dad It's their house. Have some manners.

John's Mum I'm the one with manners, Rob! I actually enjoy chatting about normal things instead of banging on about how they're moving down the road because too many Asians are moving in.

John's Dad They're not lying, are they? Look out the window.

John's Mum Oh come off it, Rob.

John's Dad I don't have a problem with anyone, but there, look. Another one.

John's Mum Another what?

John's Dad It's like Gary said. Why can't the Pakistanis play football? Cos every time they get a corner, they open a shop.

John's Mum They're just shops.

John's Dad And a few weeks ago it was just a couple of planes flying into buildings.

John's Mum Lucky we're not in America, then.

John's Dad I told you how Gary's cousin was put in hospital during the riots. That's Burnley, love. And Bradford. Not bloody . . . Baltimore. And my mates are good people. Not their fault if they weren't brought up in massive houses. Riding horses like a princess.

John's Mum My parents worked hard. They achieved.

John's Dad Oh yeah? And what have you done?

10

Busy roads and traffic speeding past.

John I could probably do this with my eyes closed. I've only been driving three years, well, four and a half-ish if you count Covid, I joined in late Covid, one of those who would never have looked twice at the job description for a delivery driver at a national supermarket based out of a warehouse off the A63 but you fast-forward like in a bad movie and suddenly here I am, still here, still in this vest, in this van, counting down the minutes until I can speed back to the yard, tap my card, bank the overtime and then

Yeah, head home probably.

The sounds of the suburbs: light wind, birds tweeting. Calming.

VO One forty-five p.m. Forty-five minutes before John approaches the Wingfield Farm roundabout.

John It's bloody nice out here, away from the hubbub, the concrete, it's clean driveways and no weeds in the gardens, there's money here but it's not showy though I've heard from some of the other drivers that they've delivered to Hull City players who bed down here, wouldn't be surprised, if you had to plant roots in this part of the world you could do worse then a detached house in Swanland and your kids on the bus to Hymers, co-ed, private, leading light in the north of England, life-changing education according to the sign outside the grounds, and I always wonder maybe if that was me, if I'd had that, if I'd applied myself, would I . . . although I did, I think, didn't I? I dunno, I always wonder what if, what if Hymers was for me, what if I'd been like Katie. Bloody hell give it a rest, John, you're bringing the mood down, try and bloody focus, it's just –

John's Dad If you're distracted, John, you're not concentrating. And if you're not concentrating, you're . . . what? John?

The van crunches on gravel, squeals to a stop.

John When you pull up, when you finally find the right house, sometimes they've got names not numbers, the silly bastards, if another person swaps number 36 for Oak House or Beech House or Time Waster's Tree House, I'll give up, so you tap your device, your device thingy and it sends a text to the customer so they know you've arrived, though usually they pretend they haven't received it so when you buzz the bell and they're up fifteen flights they play dumb and say –

Shopper 1 Gosh, you've worked up a sweat, if I'd known I'd have come down!

John And other guff like –

Shopper 2 The intercom's broken, you see, and my knee's been playing up, and didn't the drivers used to come in and actually drop the bags in the kitchen or –

John They stopped that in Covid. They know the rules. I know the rules, that's for sure, and it's to get out, unload, flash a smile, ambients in that crate, fridge and freezer goods in another, too many plastic bags of course, sorry about that, they bang on about the environment, God forbid we should idle the vans but they'll still put a bulb of garlic into a whole plastic bag and if you don't want to keep them, you know, to put in your bins or whatever, to line your bins, then just leave them in the crates and I'll take them back to the depot and I'll make sure they're chucked.

I'll make sure they're re-used. Responsibly and all that. Anything else I can help with?

I say that as I turn my back, hoping they'll take the hint, time is money, it literally is if I start running late for drops and then the other customers get pissed off because their slot is delayed and then I get the whole sob story about how –

Shopper 3 We booked an early slot because I have to get to work and she needs to visit her dad. This happens every time –

John I can't do anything about traffic, I'm so sorry, if you have any further questions or comments there's a number on your order confirmation, that'll take you through to customer services, I wish I could be of more help but unfortunately they pack in as many drops in an hourly slot as they can and it's just no guarantee, it does say that actually, there's no guarantee, but like I said I should probably get going, so I get going, I start heading to the van, sweating a shitload now I'm worried it's marking my pits, I always wash at forty for extra long, I know it should be thirty for the climate and all that but fuck me I can't be traipsing around town with stains on my tee, must top up the non-bio actually, I get them discounted in the warehouse store, it's a store just for staff, all the stuff you get on the High Street but heavily discounted, I said that already, Christ, don't be boring, John, though I always think I've beaten the system with half-price Haribo and cheddar that's cheap as chips, but then I remember they pay us fucking peanuts so am I really winning? Anyway, don't dwell, I'm nearly at the van and they've taken the bags in when –

Shopper 4 Sorry! Is this a substitution? I don't remember ordering cherry tomatoes.

John Someone's subbed chopped tomatoes with a packet of cherry tomatoes, it's bonkers when you think about it, but the pickers are a bit thick, in fact that's harsh, they're mostly just students paying their rent, probably know more about the left wing, the right wing, the triple locks than I do, but now I've got to sort this sub out and I'm nearly out of the hourly slot which means the final deliveries will be late and that'll be on my head but it's not the end of the world, I can just do this sub on my device, the device thingy, but this customer won't stop rabbiting on so I nod and smile and I can do this with my eyes closed and I wonder if I did, if I closed my eyes, if I close my eyes, when I close my eyes, I can't stop seeing Katie and her face and a look in her eye, was it pity, does she pity me, does she think I'm pathetic, was it love, maybe, I guess she might always love me in some way but we were too young, it was never proper, couldn't even last first term of uni because of her essays and societies and she started volunteering for a project, Oxbridge thing, they sent letters of support on behalf of prisoners with wrongful convictions, she was always like that, she spoke up for people, she persuaded her sixth form to un-cancel the prom, they tried to cancel the prom the cheeky buggers, tight private-school bastards, better spent elsewhere, and it was Katie who turned that around, she led the charge, I'll always remember that, she wanted me to come along, she wanted me to be her plus-one, and I was nervous, of course I was, me from her old school, the shitty comp, landing in amongst the crowd who call tea dinner and dinner lunch, with their River Island suits and their skinny ties from Next, and I did, I went with her, I took her to prom, can you believe that, the rest of our lives looking back at us saying come on then, the DJ and the dancers and Katie looking back with a grin saying, come on then, John, what have you got? I listened to so much Justin Timberlake and only she knew and I loved it when she took the piss, come on then, John, rock your body, what have you got?

11

The poppy, cheesy beats of a fun bar. John dances his arse off.

VO Humber Street. A very cool bar. One thirty a.m. Thirteen hours before John approaches the Wingfield Farm roundabout.

John Can we go outside?

Katie What?

John Can we go outside?

He dances.

Katie, can we –

Katie Yeah, yeah. I'll meet you outside.

John Do you want another?

Katie What?

John I might get myself a . . . do you want another, I said?

Katie No, no, I'm fine, I'm fine. I'll see you outside.

John I might . . . Yeah. I'll get myself another, Katie. Just a . . . Yeah.

He dances to the bar.

An Amstel. Amstel, please. Pint, yeah. Cheers.

He moves to the music. He gazes around the room.

Actually, could you get me a couple of tequilas? Yeah. Tequilas. Two. *Numero dos*. Just two, yeah, cheers.

He balances the drinks, wandering through a crowd. He bumps into someone.

Punter Watch it!

John Sorry! Sorry! All good in the hood. Apologies, *amigo* . . .

Punter Prick.

Minutes later. Outside. Distant beats.

Katie God, it's freezing. Always forget it's ten degrees colder the moment you leave London.

John How is London?

Katie Yeah, fine. It's nice. I like it.

John That's good.

Katie We're moving when we get back from honeymoon. If it all works out with the exchange of contracts and that. Could all go to shit, though.

John I'm sure it won't.

Katie You should come visit. Once we've . . . the kitchen needs doing, basically.

John Yeah. Yeah that sounds good.

Pause.

Katie How's Hull treating you, John?

John You sure you don't want this shot?

Katie I'm sure. Thanks though.

John Pinky positive?

Katie You what?

John Pinky promise? I think I meant pinky promise. Dunno what I'm saying.

Katie You're drunk, aren't you?

John I've had a couple, yeah. Is that bad?

Katie It's not bad, course it's not. It was just an observation, John.

John I'm not as pissed as Lord Farquaad.

Katie Who?

John The . . . your best mate. Posh bloke. Harry?

Katie Oh. Hadley.

John That's the one.

Katie Lord Farquaad. Haven't heard that in a while.

John Cracking film, *Shrek*.

Katie Yeah.

John I saw it with my dad. Eddie Murphy as that donkey. He was pissing himself.

Katie Hadley's not my best mate, by the way. I met him at Cambridge. His partner, Nancy? She's one of my besties. Don't know how she puts up with him.

John How about your fella?

Katie My fella?

John Yeah. Y'know . . .

Pause.

Pat . . . Martin?

Katie His name's Matthew.

John Right. Sorry. Matt.

Katie He *hates* 'Matt'. So best avoid that if you want to stay on his good side.

John Noted.

Katie It's his mum. Always saying, 'Matthew, you're not something people can wipe their shoes on!' Men and their mums, eh?

Pause.

Shit. Sorry.

John What for?

Katie I didn't . . . I'm sorry, John.

John You're fine. Sure you don't want this shot?

Katie How is she?

Pause.

John Not good. Yeah.

Pause.

It is bloody cold.

Katie What's . . . what are the hospice saying?

John Well, it's a hospice, isn't it?

Katie No, I know, I'm sorry, I phrased that badly, I'm –

John It's okay. You're fine. Thank you for asking. She'll appreciate that. She loves you. She loved you. You know that. Obviously. All of your, y'know, your smarts. And stuff. Your general . . . good. Christ, sorry. Think I am pissed.

Punters Katie! Kit! Kit! It's your song! Come on!

Katie I think I'm being summoned.

John Can I ask you something, Katie?

Katie Course. Anything.

John How do I . . . How can I . . .

Katie What?

John How do I get what you have?

Pause.

Katie John –

John No, wait, sorry, just . . . Katie, I . . . I'm up in the morning, in a few hours really, should have called it a night a while ago to be honest . . . and I'm delivering shopping. I'm delivering shopping to people. And I make some money and then I go home. But, um . . . I can afford things. I get by. Pension and that. Discount. Twelve and a half per cent off, maybe fifteen if I move into line management or whatever but . . . anyway, that's boring, just hear me out. Please. Sorry.

Katie John –

John I'd love to be like you, Katie. You did it all.

Katie I'm a civil servant, John. With a small flat in suburban London. I'm not Taylor Swift.

John No. I know. But you've done other things. I don't mean that . . . all that stuff. The signs and symbols. Assets and whatnot. I don't mean that. I'm talking bigger stuff. In . . .

With a trembling hand, he indicates his heart.

In here.

Katie Are you all right? If you're up early you should –

John You've got a lot. And maybe you had a bit more or they gave you a bit more but you've got more than you had. If that makes sense. You've got better with it. With whatever they . . . whatever they gave you at the start. But I don't think I have. I don't think they . . .

Katie Who, John?

John They don't talk about Hull, do they? They don't talk about me. They don't know who I am. They don't give a flying fuck.

Pause.

Are you sure you don't want that shot?

12

Roaring traffic. The stress of a city.

Depot Say that again for me? The line's a bit –

John I was held up, basically. The run today has been all over the shop and now there's roadworks.

VO Two twenty-six p.m. Four minutes before John approaches the Wingfield Farm roundabout.

John I was held up and then I couldn't access this block of flats and then when I did the lift was broken and –

Depot The roadworks on the A63 have been in place for a while now. There's a notice in the break room? It's laminated and in a very large, accessible font.

John Sure, yeah, but the lights never change. It's a joke. There's –

Depot We always advise drivers to check their routes.

John Listen, please, is there any way another driver could meet me? Just to take one of the final drops that are back out east because I'm heading west and –

His personal phone starts ringing.

Hold on –

He drops his personal phone in the footwell.

Oh fuck off –

Depot Beg your pardon?

John No, sorry, that wasn't –

Depot Please don't swear at me. That's not appropriate. I'm very sensitive to swearing.

John I know, I'm sorry, I know you don't like swearing –

Depot We don't tolerate any form of abuse, whether you're a customer or an employee it makes no difference –

John I just dropped my phone, all right? I just –

Depot Sorry, why are you using your phone? You're not supposed to be using your phone!

John Yeah, I know we're not supposed to use our phones. I know that. Of course I know that but –

Depot I'm not the Highway Code but use of private phones is strictly forbidden. Especially when you're in a company vehicle and therefore representing the views and ethical outlook of said company.

John You know what, actually you can fuck off.

Anita appears.

Anita I can't get there, can I? I can't just take the afternoon off, I'm on leave in a few hours, getting that signed off was a nightmare, so –

The Ex Anita, you're putting us in an impossible position –

Anita What? How?

The Ex Maya's poorly, we had to check out early, the plan was to visit a National Trust place on the way back but that was closed because of flooding, now she's got a dicky tummy so we're heading home –

Anita What did you give her to eat? Just stay at yours with her until I can get there. It's not fucking rocket science.

The Ex Calm down, Anita, and try not to swear when you're on speaker phone it's –

Anita Wait, what? Don't put me on speaker, you doughnut, I thought –

Maya MUMMY!

Anita Sweetheart, hello, hi, I didn't realise you were there –

Maya Mummy, can a bee sting a wasp?

Anita Sorry what, love?

The Ex She's asking if a bee –

Maya Can a bee sting a wasp, Mummy!

Anita I really don't know, love, but I really want to find out, how about we find out when you're home, are you feeling all right, Maya?

The Ex It's just a dicky tummy, so maybe we grab a Coke Zero from a services –

Maya I want to find out and Daddy said we could find out but now my throat is all tickly and –

Anita Right, love, just hang on, has Daddy given you any medicine yet?

The Ex I'm not a walking pharmacy, Anita, when we get home I'll sort it, as per –

Anita Oh, honest to God, don't you start, I'm at work so I –

The Ex Well, you're obviously not at work otherwise you wouldn't take this call, would you?

Anita You texted me all capitals saying ring you! All capitals like . . . like you'd fallen down a well or something!

The Ex What are you on about?

Anita What's this guy doing now, stop swerving, stupid fucking vans –

The Ex Anita!

Anita I'll call you back.

She hangs up.

Just stay in your lane, pal, bloody hell. You won't get there any faster. We're all in the same queue. Moron.

John Fucking move, man, come on!

They both turn their radios on.

They wait in traffic, listening, steadying their nerves.

They breathe, calming down.

They close their eyes.

Their phones start ringing. John tries to grab his . . .

Come here, come on . . .

Anita rejects her call . . .

Anita Go away, silly man, silly man, go away.

John's phone is still ringing as the sound of traffic gets louder, more intense. A distant car horn.

Yes, I'm moving, you idiot. Give me a second. Christ.

John Fucking let me in, man, we're both going the same way –

Anita You can't go right there you can't go right there –

John Just let me in come on –

Anita You're in the wrong lane stop fucking swerving you're –

John No no shit fucking don't no no NO NO –

CRASH. Time freezes.

Silence.

John and Anita see each other for the first time.

The sound of distant traffic returns as:

One minute. I need my . . . I need my thingy. Device. Stupid thing. Just wait there, all right? I need pictures.

His phone starts ringing.

Oh fuck off. Not now . . . not now . . . Where the fuck is it?

He finds his phone. Sees the caller ID.

Yeah, hi, sorry, I'm just in the middle of –

It's John, yeah. Speaking. I'm at work actually can I –

Sorry, what does –

No, carry on, what were you saying?

Right.

John, yeah. I'm her son.

No, I understand. I understand. I'll be there. I will. Can you, uh . . . can you tell her I'll be there? Tell her that, please.

Thank you. Yeah. And, uh . . .

Doesn't matter. I'll be there. Yeah. Okay. Thanks. Okay. Bye.

He hangs up. Turns back to Anita.

Anita Hi. Yeah. We should swap details? For insurance? I'm sorry but . . . I'm Anita. By the way.

Pause.

The left lane there, well, both lanes go straight, you can still go straight but you'd already started heading off the roundabout, you were already heading towards the bridge. And, look, I think we've all done something similar before because that sign up there, Humber Bridge, in red, all caps, no reversing, no U-turns, cameras in operation, Christ, that makes us all a bit nervous but yeah. Look, I . . .

Pause.

I'm sorry but you shouldn't have swerved like that. So, uh, let's –

John Fucking unbelievable.

Pause.

Anita Sorry?

John Look at what you've done. Don't you understand? Look at what –

Anita I didn't –

John This is what happens when people don't know how to drive. This is what happens. But no, don't worry, you stand there looking gormless and hopeless and helpless. Look at what you've done. And I can't leave, can I? No. Can't drive off and keep calm and carry on cos it'll be me that has to fill in the forms and submit the claims and prove my bloody innocence because they'll assume I'm fucking guilty because . . . what? Eh? Because I was late? Because I struggle to maintain the optimal chilling temperature in the fridge?

Anita Sorry. I –

John Well, no wonder, I say, because the way these fucking vans are designed they only get cold when the engine's running and half the time the engine's off because I'm climbing ten flights of stairs in a piss-stained tower and if I try and swing it, if I try and take a chance, what happens? Eh? They call me in for a one-to-one, don't they? Why've you been idling, John? Why you've been sat on the side of the road just running the engine? Why the fucking hell do you think I'm idling?! I'm always idling. At work, before work, on the way to work, I'm idling. Bone fucking idle, me. But you can't put that in a report, can you? No. Can't report that to the loss adjuster. The ombudsman. The relevant authorities. Can't blame it on anyone else but me. It's my fault, as per. Despite it all, despite the evidence, it's my fucking fault. And I'm tired of it. All right? I'm sick and bloody tired.

Anita Sorry but you can't talk to me like that. Okay? I'm going to –

John I'll talk to you how I fucking want.

Pause. Anita goes to say something, then stops.

I'll talk to you how I fucking want. Standing there, staring, thinking you know me. You don't know me.

Anita I'm going back to my car now.

She begins to move.

John You don't know me.

Anita I'm contacting your employer and we'll deal with it that way.

John But I sure as hell know you. I know your kind.

Anita freezes.

You stupid fucking Pak—

He doesn't say the whole word. But it's enough. It changes the world.

13

John begins to change out of his delivery driver outfit and back into the cheap suit.

John You need to know
   That when that Nissan Micra clipped my bumper on the Wingfield Farm Roundabout, just after the junction with the A15

I saw red
The traffic lights up ahead were green then orange
I saw red
The leaves on the dirty trees by the side of that busy road were autumnal and orange
I could only see red

And then I saw her

She got out slowly, bemused
And I couldn't stop seeing red
And she was brown
And I couldn't stop remembering that I was really very late and that I was on two formal warnings and that a third would render my position untenable
And I couldn't have that
Not today in this world of a bank account with no interest and my hands to my mouth and no fucking chance of anything unless I'm black and gay and brown and deaf
When all I want is a chance

I'm nothing
I have nothing
I didn't have much but now I have nothing
And I didn't mean it
I didn't mean what I said and I didn't mean what I did but I did it

I gave her a chance and she didn't take it
She clipped my bumper and now I'd be late and she still didn't
Fucking Understand
So I told her to Understand
And she looked at me
The strangest of flickers
Like that boy in the blue blazer with the smirk on his face
And she said
Don't talk me to like that
She didn't understand

She said
Don't talk to me like that
And I saw red and I said
I'll talk to you how I fucking want

And her face turned and I could see she was scared now
I'll talk to you how I fucking want
And as her face turned I saw her but I also saw Dad

He broke me into pieces and didn't put me back again
And then I saw Mum
And I saw

I saw red and then brown but I've helped the homeless
I've helped refugees for fuck's sake and I can't explain it

But she was so slow and confused and it's not her or her skin or that look on her face but Christ on a bike I swear I've done good things in my time

I have done good things

But when that Nissan Micra clipped my bumper on the Wingfield Farm roundabout, just after the junction with the A15

I was in a rush

You need to know that.

Pause.

Lawyer So the thing is, John, I can't actually answer questions in the tribunal about specific circumstances that may or may not be relevant to your case. Hopefully you've had a chance to peruse the documents in the bundle?

John I have. Yeah.

Lawyer Good. So as long as you're familiar with all that, then you just need to make sure you have your documents, witness statements, chronology of events, any compensation demands, your questions for the employer's witnesses, and we should be good to go.

John Okay.

Lawyer Lovely jubbly. I'm just gonna nip to the gents, all right?

John Okay. I might have a quick vape. Out there, obviously. Before we –

Lawyer No bother. Enjoy.

14

Anita in the car park, at work, surveying.
   She scratches the back of her neck. She gets out a tube of moisturising cream and carefully applies it to her skin. It maybe stings a bit.
   John enters from another side of the car park, with his vape and bundle of documents.
   A moment as they see each other.

Anita I had a flare-up. Shame, really. Did you know they want to turn this into flats?

   Pause.

John No. I . . . That's nice.

Anita Is it?

John I dunno.

Anita Rip-off flats or rip-off car parks? What's the lesser evil?

   Pause.

What are you . . . ?

John Tribunal. Employment. Constructive dismissal.

Anita Right.

John I –

Anita No.

John What?

Anita Don't.

John Okay.

Anita You'll spoil the view. Look.

John What about it?

Anita Not bad, is it?

John I suppose.

Anita The water.

John Yeah.

Pause.

Anita That's how it is, by the way. In case you were wondering. It's like water. Or waves. It's like –

Radio Two were flown into the Twin Towers of the World Trade Center in New York, a third into the Pentagon, and a fourth crashed after passengers tackled the hijackers.

Anita Like high tide and low tide, pushing out to the horizon and drifting back again, splashing and crashing, rippling, slow, sometimes deadly, mankind in cahoots with nature, the thrust and pull of the gods putting you back in your place.

Radio A report by a former social worker revealed that an estimated fourteen hundred children had been sexually abused in the town from 1997 to 2013, predominantly by British Pakistani men.

Anita Because it's always there. We just don't take much notice if it's calm and considered and carefully insidious. It's at bay sometimes, when things are good, when you smile at a stranger, when someone lets you cross the road, when you dance with abandon, when you laugh with a crowd, when you see your child, when you think of your family, when you get that job, when someone thinks kindly of you, when the universe and its gravitational rules keep the waters in check and the sunshine flowing, but like waves –

Radio Men can be seen throwing bricks and a shopping trolley at the car. Another man can be seen performing the Nazi salute.

Anita It can properly fuck you up and turn a holiday into a horror film, it can stab the sides of your body in ways you didn't know you could be hit, it can take you back to Freshney Place, age thirteen, with your mum in her sari even though you beg, you *beg* her to stop wearing fucking saris and you get that pack of Monster Munch which you've been craving for hours but you cross paths with those girls in the year above with too much make-up and too many spotty boys hovering around like fleas drunk on Lynx Africa and you want to take the wave that comes, because it always comes, and you wanna grab it with both hands, with your arms and legs and claws, and beg to be taken under, you want to be swallowed, to dive, to die, to be safely stowed away until you're an adult by some spectacular hocus-pocus and now things are in your hands, they say, it's your game to play, it's winner takes all and you don't need to worry about the aches and pains of sleepovers when your house smells funny, your sweet unknowing parents with their not quite right accents, now you're a grown-up and able to take on any wave that comes with the experience and capability of a surfer down under, but the waves still come, it'll be surprising sometimes, like visiting your mum and loving the way she dresses and hating yourself for ever wanting her to disappear, the man you dream of and walking into places and seeing faces turn and not being able to tell him your innermost fears, the things that keep you from keeping on for fear he'll just think you're making it up, that some people are just less friendly than others, that all pubs in the countryside are a bit weird, love, that an anxiety can thicken can get mouldy can be deep-fat-fried like a chip, can weigh down your shoulders and leave you shuddering –

Radio Sophie Dickie in Lincoln, there was also Tom Bellenden in Scunthorpe –

Maya Mummy, can a bee sting a wasp?

GP Are you experiencing any stress at the moment?

Pause.

Anita It is stressful, pal. To say the fucking least. It's heavy. It's physical, a proper work-out, it's a conundrum that I'm always trying my hardest *to* work out, because no matter what, regardless of the rules and the relentless refusal to stick out, there are men – and women to be fair, quite a few of them too, let's not be sexist – who will not let you forget the lay of the land, and it's not about Labour or Tories or two tiers or one rule for them, another for us, it's the relentless refusal to accept the fact that sometimes it's just so fucking unfair and you need to blame someone, we always need to find someone to bloody blame because it's painful, isn't it? It's knackering. I'm *tired*, so are you by the looks of things, we're basically in the same boat for ninety-nine per cent of the time, but there's that subtle, shitty one per cent, there's the rest of it which doesn't let up, when the boat is so violently rocked, and it might be your mum, it might be your dad, it might be your job, but whatever it is, you're feeling sad and you see someone like me and that's when it all clicks, when it makes sense. But it doesn't, it's nonsense really, it makes no sense at all, it's confused, it's warped, it's deeply fundamentally and profoundly disturbed, that's when you see me and I see you and there is a choice to be made and you fucking made it. Your boat was rocked and you struck me like a fucking wave. What was the bloody point of that?

Pause.

John I . . .

Anita Go on.

John I don't know. I don't. I'm not sure.

Anita None of us are, really. Ever. But that's not an excuse.

Pause.

There are no excuses. Am I making sense?

John nods.

Because it shouldn't have to be me. It doesn't need to be anyone, really. You should just . . . not say those kinds of things. Because, at the end of the day, we're all just fucking trying.

Pause.

Can I ask you something? Before your, uh . . . ?

John Tribunal.

Anita That's the one. What did you think?

John About . . . ?

Anita When they rioted?

Pause.

John It was sad. I was sad.

Anita Who for?

Pause.

John This city . . . It isn't that.

Anita What is it, then?

John considers. Anita waits, watches him.

He goes to say something, and then hesitates.

Nothing.

Anita exits.

John, alone.

He places his bundle of documents on a ledge. He looks at his vape.

And then he looks out.

Towards the city.

The bridge.

The water.